Curt Schilling

By Jeffrey Zuehlke

AMAZING
ATHLETES

Lerner Publications Company • Minneapolis

For Freddie, Chris, C. J., and the rest of the Fenway Faithful

Lerner Publications Company
A division of Lerner Publishing Group
241 First Avenue North
Minneapolis, MN 55401 U.S.A.

Website address: www.lernerbooks.com

Library of Congress Cataloging-in-Publication Data

Zuehlke, Jeffrey, 1968-
    Curt Schilling / by Jeffrey Zuehlke.
      p.   cm.—(Amazing athletes)
    Includes index.
    ISBN-13: 978-0-8225-3431-0 (lib. bdg. : alk. paper)
    ISBN-10: 0-8225-3431-2 (lib. bdg. : alk. paper)
    1. Schilling, Curt—Juvenile literature. 2. Baseball players—United States—Juvenile literature. I. Title. II. Series.
    GV865.S353Z84 2007
    796.357'092—dc22   2005017970

Manufactured in the United States of America
1 2 3 4 5 6 – DP – 12 11 10 09 08 07

TABLE OF CONTENTS

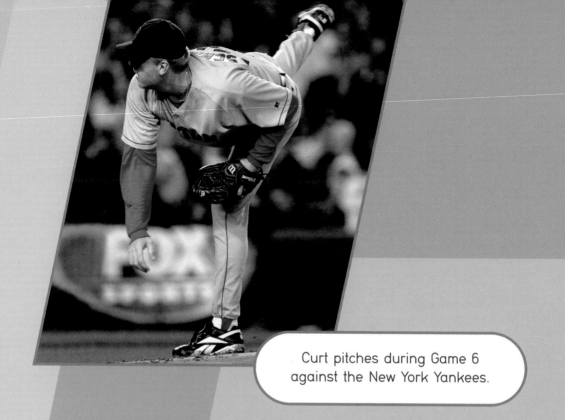

Curt pitches during Game 6 against the New York Yankees.

PITCHING IN PAIN

Boston Red Sox pitcher Curt Schilling threw a blazing **fastball** toward home plate. New York Yankees shortstop Derek Jeter swung hard at the pitch. Jeter hit a high fly ball to right field. Red Sox right fielder Trot Nixon caught the ball for the first out of the game.

Curt's Red Sox were battling the Yankees in Game 6 of the 2004 **American League Championship Series.** More than 55,000 fans had filled Yankee Stadium. They were hoping to see the Yankees beat the Red Sox to earn a trip to the **World Series.**

But Curt had other ideas. Days earlier, he had pitched badly in Game 1 of the series. His right ankle was hurt, and he had given up six runs in just three innings. The Yankees won the game, 10–7. Then they went on to clobber the Red Sox in the next two games. The Yankees took a 3–0 lead in the series.

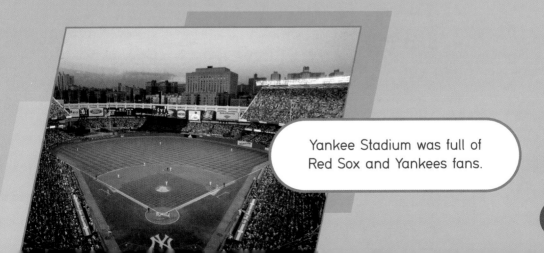

Yankee Stadium was full of Red Sox and Yankees fans.

Curt and the Red Sox were discouraged during Game 1 of the American League Championship Series.

Boston's dreams of getting to the World Series seemed dead. No team in baseball history had won a series after losing the first three games. But Curt's team refused to give up. They fought back to win Games 4 and 5.

Boston Red Sox fans are known as Red Sox Nation.

The Red Sox and their fans turned to Curt for Game 6. Doctors had stitched up his ankle. But would he be able to pitch? TV cameras zoomed in on Curt's ankle. A red bloodstain had already appeared on Curt's white sock. Could Curt stand the pain? And could he beat the Yankees' superstar hitters? The Yankees had great sluggers like Jeter, third baseman Alex Rodriguez, right fielder Gary Sheffield, and left fielder Hideki Matsui.

Yankee's star hitter Derek Jeter was a challenge for the Red Sox.

Curt's right ankle was bleeding,
but he ignored the pain.

Curt soon showed that he could beat the Yankees. He ignored the pain in his ankle. He threw great pitch after great pitch. The Yankees couldn't score for the first six innings. Meanwhile, the Red Sox scored four runs in the fourth inning to take the lead. Curt gave up one run in the seventh, but that was it.

The Red Sox won, 4–2. After the game, everyone talked about Curt's courage and toughness. "I don't think any of us have any idea what he went through out there," said Red Sox manager Terry Francona. "His heart is so big. He made it happen."

The Red Sox needed just one win to complete the greatest comeback in baseball history. They were one win away from the World Series. Could they do it?

Curt was born in
Anchorage, Alaska.

POWER ARM

Curtis Montague Schilling was born on
November 14, 1966, in Anchorage, Alaska.
Curt's father, Cliff, served in the U.S. Army.
Curt's mother's name is Mary. He has an older
sister named Allison.

Cliff Schilling was a big baseball fan. After
Curt was born, Cliff put a baseball glove in
Curt's crib. He wanted his son to grow up to

love the game too.

The Schilling family moved around a lot. As a boy, Curt lived in Kentucky, Illinois, and Missouri. His family finally settled in Paradise Valley, near Scottsdale, Arizona.

Arizona's warm weather allowed Curt to play sports year-round. His favorite game was baseball.

Curt's dad grew up in Pennsylvania. His favorite teams were the Pittsburgh Pirates in baseball and the Pittsburgh Steelers in football. Curt grew to love those teams too.

By the time he reached high school, Curt had a very strong arm. He could throw the ball very hard and very far.

In 1984, after Curt's **junior year** in high school, he went to a **tryout camp** with the Cincinnati Reds.

Curt wowed the Reds **scouts** with his strong arm. He threw the ball 90 miles per hour! This was very fast for a high school pitcher.

The Reds liked Curt's talent. The only problem was that Curt was just 17 years old. He was too young to become a professional baseball player. Still, Curt was excited to learn that he might be a successful pitcher one day.

Curt graduated from high school in 1985. He went to Yavapai Junior College in Arizona. He was one of the best pitchers on the team. In

Curt *(back row, second from right)* poses with his baseball team in 1984.

his first season, he won 11 games and lost only 3.

The Boston Red Sox liked Curt's strong arm. They selected him in the January 1986 baseball **draft.** He signed a **contract** for $20,000. He was just 19 years old. Curt was going to become a professional baseball player! But was he good enough to make the **major leagues**?

Curt is one of only eight people born in Alaska to make it to the major leagues.

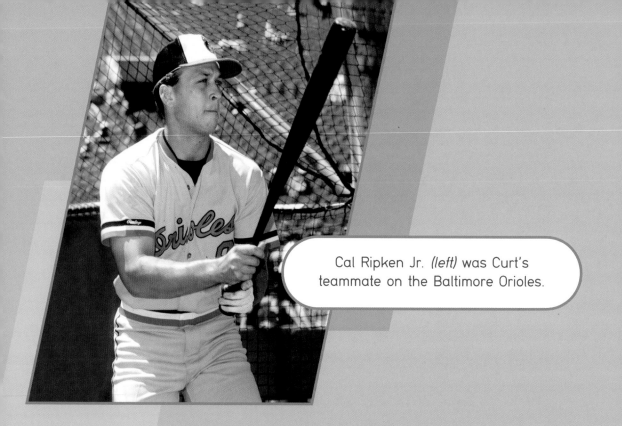

Cal Ripken Jr. *(left)* was Curt's teammate on the Baltimore Orioles.

UPS AND DOWNS

Like most players, Curt started his pro career
in the **minor leagues**. His first team was the
Elmira Pioneers of Elmira, New York. In his
first season, Curt won 7 games and lost only 3.
He also had a very good **earned run average
(ERA)** of 2.59.

The next year, he struck out 189 hitters in just 184 innings. The Baltimore Orioles liked Curt's pitching. In July 1988, the Orioles traded for Curt.

The Orioles were a losing team. They thought Curt could help them. Near the end of the 1988 season, the Orioles called up Curt to pitch in the major leagues. He joined an Orioles team that included superstar shortstop Cal Ripken Jr.

Curt pitched well in his first major-league **start**. The Orioles won the game, 4–3. But Curt pitched poorly the rest of the season. He lost three games in a row.

Curt had the talent to become a good pitcher. But he didn't take his job very seriously. His coaches wondered if Curt was willing to work hard enough to be the best.

The Orioles played at Memorial Stadium in Baltimore, Maryland, until 1992.

Curt had a lot of growing up to do. The Orioles traded him to the Houston Astros before the 1991 season. Curt pitched for the Astros in 1991. Sometimes he did great. Most of the time, however, he pitched badly.

Finally, Curt realized he needed to work harder. He spent the **off-season** working out every day. The next spring, he came to the Astros ready to be a winner.

But the Astros traded Curt to the Philadelphia Phillies. He pitched for the Phillies in 1992. Curt had his best season yet. He won 14 games. He had a super ERA of just 2.35. But the team finished in last place. Still, Curt had shown he could be a star.

Curt played for the Houston Astros in 1991.

The next year, Curt and the Phillies did much better. Curt won 16 games. The team won 97 games. Curt's great pitching helped the Phillies beat the Atlanta Braves in the 1993 National League Championship Series. The Phillies played the Toronto Blue Jays in the World Series. But the Phillies lost to Toronto in six thrilling games. Curt hoped to win it all the next year.

Curt pitches in the 1993 World Series.

Curt and the Phillies struggled after the 1993 World Series.

GOING HOME

Curt and the Phillies never made it back to the World Series. Instead, the team struggled. Curt struggled too. He had problems with his elbow, knee, and shoulder.

When Curt was healthy, he pitched great. He won 17 games in 1997 and 15 games in 1998. He struck out a whopping 300 or more batters both seasons.

But the Phillies kept losing. By 2000, Curt was ready for a change. In July, the Phillies traded him to the Arizona Diamondbacks. Curt was excited. He was going to play near the city where he grew up. And he was joining a great team. The D-Backs had power-hitting outfielders Luis Gonzalez and Steve Finley. And Curt would also be teaming up with hard-throwing left-handed pitcher Randy Johnson.

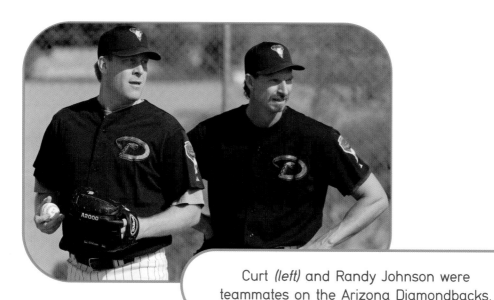

Curt *(left)* and Randy Johnson were teammates on the Arizona Diamondbacks.

Curt winds up for a pitch. His pitching helped take the Diamondbacks to the World Series in 2001.

The D-Backs didn't make the playoffs in 2000. But the next season, Curt and Randy led the D-Backs all the way to the World Series.

Arizona faced a powerful Yankees team. But Curt and Randy knew they could beat anyone. Curt blew away the Yankees in Game 1. The D-Backs won, 9–1. Then Randy helped the team win Game 2 by a score of 4–0. But the Yankees stormed back to win the next three games and take a lead in the series. After Randy won Game 6, it was all up to Curt.

Curt pitched well in Game 7. But the Yankees managed to take a 2–1 lead into the ninth inning. All seemed lost until the D-Backs scored 2 runs in the bottom of the ninth for an exciting win. The D-Backs were world champions!

"I just hope that was as fun to watch as it was to play in," said Curt. "Because that's got to be one of the greatest World Series ever played."

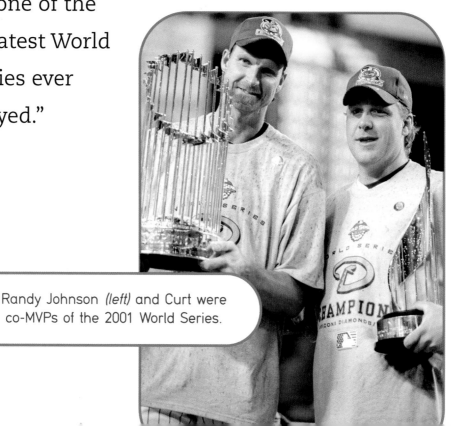

Randy Johnson *(left)* and Curt were co-MVPs of the 2001 World Series.

Curt watches his team during a game against the Los Angeles Dodgers in 2002.

BACK TO BOSTON

Curt had another amazing season in 2002. He won 23 games and struck out more than 300 batters. The D-Backs made the playoffs but lost to the St. Louis Cardinals.

In 2003, Curt struggled with injuries and the D-Backs didn't make the playoffs. By this time, the D-Backs were ready to make a change. They agreed to trade Curt to the Boston Red Sox.

Curt was thrilled to go back to the team that had drafted him 17 years earlier. And he was eager to take on Boston's biggest rival, the mighty Yankees. "I like the thought of playing in the biggest rivalry in sports in front of some incredible fans," said Curt.

Red Sox fans were thrilled too. They had waited 86 years to win a World Series. Could Curt help them finally win it all?

Curt showed that he could. He was one of the best pitchers in the league in 2004. He won 21 games. The Red Sox won 98 games and earned a spot in the playoffs. They defeated the Anaheim Angels in the American League **Division Series.** Then they faced the Yankees. After Curt's great win in Game 6, the Red Sox pounded the Yankees in Game 7. Boston won 10–3. The incredible comeback was complete.

Curt pitched well throughout the 2004 season. Here he pitches against the Kansas City Royals at Fenway Park.

In the World Series, Boston faced the powerful St. Louis Cardinals. The Cardinals had won more games than any other team in 2004. And they had a bunch of hard-hitting sluggers, including Albert Pujols, Jim Edmonds, and Scott Rolen.

Each year, the Cy Young Award is given to the best pitcher in each league. Curt has never won the award. But he has finished in second place several times.

But the Red Sox were unstoppable. They beat up on the Cardinals to earn a 4–0 **sweep.** The Red Sox were world champions! "Now they can rejoice in the city of Boston,"

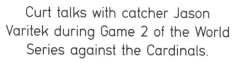

Curt talks with catcher Jason Varitek during Game 2 of the World Series against the Cardinals.

Curt rides in a parade celebrating Boston's World Series victory. Two of his children ride with him.

said Curt's teammate, pitcher Tim Wakefield. Most of Boston and New England celebrated. "I'm so proud of being a part of the greatest Red Sox team in history," said Curt.

A few days later, Curt had surgery on his ankle. "The bottom line is to get back to the World Series and win it," Curt said.

Curt's second season with the Red Sox was hard. His ankle was still not fully healed. He made only 11 starts in 2005.

Curt tips his hat to fans after getting his 3,000th career strikeout in 2006.

Curt pitched in a few games as a reliever for the first time since 1992. The Red Sox made the playoffs. But they lost in the Division Series to the Chicago White Sox.

Curt went after one of baseball's all-time records in 2006. At a game in Oakland in August, Curt recorded his 3,000th strikeout. He is just the 14th pitcher in baseball history to reach 3,000 strikeouts.

The Red Sox missed the playoffs in 2006. But more chances await the team with Curt leading the way. Through 19 up-and-down professional seasons, he has proven himself to be one of baseball's best and toughest pitchers.

Selected Career Highlights

2006 Recorded 3,000th strikeout
Finished third in the American League in
  strikeouts

2005 Passed Mickey Lolich for 16th place on all-time
  strikeout list

2004 Helped lead Boston Red Sox to first World
Series title since 1918
Led Major League Baseball in wins with a
  21–6 record
Named to All-Star team for the sixth time

2003 Posted a 2.95 ERA, fifth best in the National League
Pitched 3 complete games, including 2 shutouts
Struck out 195 batters, fifth best in the National League

2002 Won a career-high 23 games
Struck out more than 300 batters for the third time in his career
Named starting pitcher for the National League All-Star team

2001 Helped lead Arizona Diamondbacks to the World Series
  championship
Named World Series co-Most Valuable Player with Randy Johnson
Received the Roberto Clemente Award for public service
Finished second to Randy Johnson in voting for the National
  League Cy Young Award
Finished the season with a 22–6 record, a 2.98 ERA, and 6
  complete games
Struck out 293 hitters, second most in the National League

2000 Traded from Philadelphia Phillies to Arizona Diamondbacks
Pitched 8 complete games, including 2 shutouts
Struck out 168 batters

1999 Finished the season with a 15–6 record and a 3.54 ERA
Pitched 8 complete games
Named starting pitcher for the National League All-Star team

1998 Struck out 300 batters, best in the National League
Led the National League in complete games with 15
Led the National League in innings pitched with 268.2
Named to the National League All-Star team

1997   Finished season with a 17–11 record and a 2.97 ERA
Struck out a Major League-high 319 batters
Named to the National League All-Star team

1993   Finished season with a 16–7 record and a 4.02 ERA
Helped lead Philadelphia Phillies to World Series
Named Most Valuable Player of the National League Championship
Series

1986   Drafted by the Boston Red Sox in the second round of the
January 1986 draft

Glossary

American League Championship Series: a seven-game series played by the winners of the two American League Division Series. The team that wins four games in the series becomes the American League champion. That team plays the National League champion in the World Series.

complete games: games in which a pitcher pitches every inning

contract: a written agreement between a player and a team

Division Series: the first round of Major League Baseball's playoffs. Teams play a five-game series. The first team to win three games moves on to the League Championship Series.

draft: an event where sports teams choose players

earned run average (ERA): a statistic that shows how many runs a pitcher has allowed per nine innings pitched. For example, if a pitcher pitches nine innings and gives up three runs, the pitcher's ERA would be 3.00

fastball: a fast pitch that usually travels straight

junior year: the third year in high school or college

major leagues: the two top North American baseball leagues, the National League and the American League

minor leagues: the baseball leagues where most baseball players begin their careers

off-season: the time between seasons

reliever: a pitcher who pitches in the later innings of a baseball game

scouts: people who watch and judge athletes' skills

start: the job of pitching from the beginning, or start, of a baseball game

sweep: to win every game in a series

tryout camp: an event in which a major league team invites players to show their skills

World Series: a set of games played each season between the best American League team and the best National League team. The winner of the World Series is the champion of Major League Baseball for that season.

Further Reading & Websites

Christopher, Matt. *On the Mound with . . . Curt Schilling.* Boston: Little, Brown and Company, 2004.

Hagen, Paul. *Curt Schilling: Phillie Phire!* Champaign, IL: Sports Publishing, 1999.

Kelley, James. *Baseball.* New York: DK Publishing, 2005.

Espn.com
http://espn.com
Espn.com covers all the major professional sports, including Major League Baseball.

Official Boston Red Sox site
http://boston.redsox.mlb.com/NASApp/mlb/index.jsp?c_id=bos
The official site of the Boston Red Sox has up-to-date news and statistics for the team.

Official MLB site
http://www.mlb.com
The official site of Major League Baseball provides up-to-date news and statistics of all 30 major-league teams and every major-league player.

Sports Illustrated for Kids
http://www.sikids.com
The *Sports Illustrated for Kids* website covers all sports, including baseball.

Index

Photo Acknowledgments

Photographs are used with the permission of: © Rob Tringali/
SportsChrome, pp. 4, 5, 6, 25, 26, 29; © Jeff Zelevansky/Icon SMI, p. 7;
© Ray Stubblebine/Reuters/CORBIS, p. 8; © Lloyd Cluff/CORBIS, p. 10;
Shadow Mountain High School, Bull's Eye 1985, p. 12; © Ron
Wyatt/SportsChrome, p. 14; © Paul A. Souders/CORBIS, p. 16; © Otto Greule
Jr./Getty Images, p. 17; AP Images/Rusty Kennedy, p. 18; AP Images/Ed
Reinke, p. 19; © Reuters/CORBIS, p. 20; © Michael Zito/SportsChrome, pp.
21, 23; © John Biever/SI/Icon SMI, p. 22; © Mike Segar/Reuters/CORBIS, p. 24;
Brian Babineau/Boston Red Sox, p. 27; © Jed Jacobson/Getty Images, p. 28.

Cover: © Rob Tringali/SportsChrome